Oahu Travel Guide

*Experience Only the Best
Places to Stay, Eat, Drink,
Hike, Bike, Beach, Surf,
Snorkel, and Discover
in Oahu, Hawaii*

by Oscar Kahekalau

Table of Contents

Introduction

Oahu is the third largest Hawaiian island, but it's the most densely populated, as it houses the state capital at Honolulu — the biggest city on the island chain. Home to more than 85% of Hawaii's population, locals appropriately call their home "The Gathering Place."

Legend has it that the islands were collectively named after the Polynesian navigator who discovered them, Hawai'iloa. The other islands were named after each of his sons, and one of them was Oahu.

Roughly diamond-shaped and divided by a chain of mountains, Oahu was formed by two shield volcanoes. This means that the lava they formed is mostly fluid, allowing it to spill below and form the main valley in the middle, and the two narrower ones facing the sea on either side. Think of a capital "M." The Waianae Range dominates the western half, while the Ko'olau Range forms the eastern portion and was made a National Natural Landmark in 1972.

The entire island is so spectacularly dramatic, that citizens don't bother with the cardinal points like everyone else in the world does. When referring to the western part of Oahu, they say "ehwa" (pronounced eh-va), which means "crooked" or "ill-fitting," because that's exactly what it looks like. Do note, however, that Ehwa is also the name of a city in the west. If you hear "Diamond Head," it refers to the eastern portion.

It gets even more interesting from here on out. "Makai" (pronounced ma-kigh) means "towards the sea," regardless of what direction it's at. When you hear this word, it obviously means that you're inland.

"Mauka" (pronounced mow-kah) can mean towards the mountains — any one of a number of them, the implication being that you're in one of the valleys. Mauka, however, can also mean "heading towards the inland," the implication being that you're on any of the beaches.

Fascinating, isn't it? The same can be said about Oahu and all it has to offer. There's Waikiki, which contains some of the most expensive real estate in the world; there's Pearl Harbor, though thank goodness the Japanese are no longer belligerent; there's spectacular scenery; and of course, there's the beaches and all the bare bodies to ogle (though some would be better off covered, admittedly).

Tourism is the island's main industry, so whether its nature you're after, city life with its clubs and shops, or something to do with culture, Oahu has it and more. Do bear in mind that the island is crowded and imports much of its stuff, making prices generally more expensive than on the US mainland. That aside, Oahu is an island paradise you should visit at least once in your life.

Chapter 1: Planning an Unforgettable Oahu Getaway

Of all the Hawaiian Islands, Oahu enjoys the most rainfall, averaging about 200 days of rain a year. From November to March it is the wet season, with temperatures averaging about 78°F (that's 25.5°C for our cousins across the pond). The months of April to October is the dry season, as the sun shines throughout, but average daytime temperatures soar to about 85°F (29.44°C).

For those who love the sea, you should know that not all of Oahu's beaches are safe for swimmers. Rip tides, currents, and high waves can be dangerous for even the strongest and most experienced swimmers. What's bad for them, however, is great for surfers.

If you are a surfer, the North Shore is world-renowned for producing waves as high as 20 to 30 feet. These batter the north from December to February. Even if you're not into surfing, it's certainly worth watching and being there. International surfing competitions are held at the North Shore during this time, so that means crowds and plenty of partying.

The Christmas season is another peak, especially for those tired of winter's chill. While a number of Asian countries do not observe the religious occasion, most do enjoy holidays at this time. With many ASEAN regions still booming despite (or perhaps because of the Global Economic Crisis), that makes it even busier.

April and early May is when the islands get packed with Japanese tourists. They call this the "Golden Week" because Japan enjoys three separate holidays, though many of them just take it in one go and skip work completely.

Finally, there's the summer vacation throughout the northern hemisphere, bringing in students from the US, Canada, and Europe. It is from June to August that the entire island of Oahu, not just the capital at Honolulu, gets packed with people and their kids.

The cost of accommodations and other things soar through the roof during these times. If money is no object to you, then congratulations — you must have great karma. Hopefully, your karma also extends to making reservations, because you'll need to book in advance if you want to do more than sleep in a tent.

If you're not one of those lucky few, then you might want to plan your itinerary accordingly.

Spring is one of the best times to go. April to May is when the weather is best — not too hot, but not too much rain and gloomy skies. May is high school graduation season, when the whole place gets filled with lei-bedecked kids celebrating the hiatus before college.

While they tend to be everywhere, their numbers do not come close to the peak seasons. You'll know that it's peak because more than half of the island's population comes from somewhere else and all are determined to cut in line before you or get in your way.

Fall, from September to November, is another great time as far as the weather is concerned. It's still warm and the days are still long, but it's the calm before the storm. Locals are either getting ready for the influx or waiting for their bonuses so they can leave. The closer you get to December, though, the more prices start edging upward.

This applies to even the room you've been occupying, so be warned. Many hotels, especially the higher end ones, do not bother to let you know that the rate you've been enjoying will go up the next day. Make sure to clarify your tariff rates or be ready to fork out a bit more when it's time to settle the bill.

Spring and fall are therefore the best times to go, if you're on a budget. With many hotel rooms and plane seats empty, expect discount fares and hotel promotions galore. Car rental prices also plummet, as do a number of tickets for certain attractions.

To fill those plane seats and hotel rooms up, various companies also offer discount packages. If you're lucky, a number of 5-star hotels and resorts will be included in their promo. The hope is that by getting you in their glamorous (but empty) rooms, you'll spend in their restaurants and shops so they can stay in business till those with real money (and great karma) come by again.

Perhaps the best thing about visiting Oahu (and the other Hawaiian islands) during the off-peak seasons is that reservations and advanced bookings are rarely necessary.

That said, what's cheap in Oahu is not the same thing as cheap on the US mainland. Home grown tropical fruits and vegetables are cheaper, but that's about it. Since most everything else is shipped from the mainland, the cost of transport will be reflected in the purchase price.

If you eat at chain restaurants and fast food outlets like McDonalds, however, the prices will be the same. Shopping at grocery stores, on the other hand, will set you back dearly. The average Hawaiian supermarket bill is 66% higher than on the mainland.

If you're not staying too long, bring over what you can. If you do stay longer, shop at chain stores like Costco, Wal-Mart, or Sam's Club to keep prices down; though you do have to purchase in bulk to make a dent in that 66% overhead.

Chapter 2: Choosing the Right Place to Stay

Unlike many of the other islands, Oahu has a lot of accommodation choices, ranging from resorts, condo rentals, hostels, budget rooms, and even campsites. If its resorts and hotels you're after, most are found in Waikiki, which offers the widest variety of budget options. The further away from Honolulu you get, the less your options and budget choices become.

BED & BREAKFASTS

If you like the idea of moving about instead of being stuck in the same place because of your package deal, a B&B is a great way to go. Normally hosting people for only a single night or two, these are often intimate mom-and-pop run places that offer a little more personality and that extra personal touch. There are others more high-end, of course, but that's up to you.

Oahu has plenty of both throughout. Whether it's something functional in the city you're after, a romantic and cozy getaway with a view of mountains or beaches, or even on some historic estate, the island has them. The following have consistently received great reviews.

Honolulu

This is the state's capital and one of the most densely packed in the world. Its name means either "sheltered harbor" or "calm port," which explains why it's an important commercial hub. It isn't all high-rise buildings, however. Honolulu, like most cities, is made up of many neighborhoods, each with its own distinct personality and style.

Manoa Valley Inn is in a quiet and less hectic part of the city, right beside the University of Hawaii. Built in 1912, it's a historic landmark built and decorated in the Victorian style (even though that era ended in 1901). It's quite posh, admittedly, with prices ranging from $160 to $245 a night, depending on the season and the choice of room. Well worth it, though, for a genuine slice of history — albeit English, not Hawaiian.

The **Aloha B&B** has no website, but they consistently rank among the top B&Bs in Honolulu. Phyllis and Don run it, including breakfast in the cost of your stay. The view from this house in Hawaii Kai is magnificent, overlooking Koko Head and the Lagoons. You can call them at (808)-518-3950 and 808-389-6694, or email them at alohaphyllis@hawaii.rr.com.

J&B's Haven B&B is also in Hawaii Kai with equally beautiful views, a mere 10 miles east of the city proper. Joan and Barbara run it in a quiet neighborhood minutes away from shops and restaurants. J&B's Haven is a stone's throw away from Sandy Beach (mostly surfers because of the waves) and Makapuu Beach.

Diamond Head B&B is run by Joane with a great view of Waikiki and Kapiolani Park without the noise and bustle, complete with garden and breakfast. It's in an upscale, quiet neighborhood, minutes from various attractions, even without a car.

Rainbow Inn is in the Aiea district with a fantastic view of Pearl Harbor and about 30 minutes away from Waikiki. The place has its own pool for those who can't wait to hit the water, as well as a beautiful garden.

Kailua

This small beach town means "two seas" or "two currents," aptly named because it's a peninsula with two lagoons running through Kailua Bay. Although it is a quiet residential town, it's also home to Lanikai Beach, the Kawai Nui Marsh, and Maunawili Falls. It also hosts the Marine Corps Base Hawaii, but that's not a tourist spot for obvious reasons.

Kailua is a beach town about half an hour's drive (traffic willing) to the northeast of Honolulu. If you do go, make sure to stop by Kailua Pali, the cliff overlooking the town and sea beyond. The view is simply breathtaking.

Kailua Beach Park was deemed to be "America's Best Beach" in 1998. It has options for swimmers, surfers, kayakers, and sailboard enthusiasts. Despite its laid-back, small town atmosphere, Kailua gets tons of visitors year round. This means that the restaurant, nightlife, and shopping options are world class. This town has hosted US President Barack Obama every year since 2008, and it was here where he signed two acts into law.

Lanikai Beach Rentals offers several choices in Kailua and Lanikai Beach. They also offer tour packages and other tourist services that can make things a lot easier for you.

Manu Mele (which means Bird Song) is another must-stay. Though officially a B&B, they offer a variety of studio apartments complete with private kitchens, gardens, and a pool. Best of all, Manu Mele is right beside the beach.

Papaya Paradise B&B is about half a mile from the beach in a quiet, residential neighborhood. There are only two rooms available and breakfast is self-service. The owners,

Bob and Jeanette, are great hosts, and their reviews have been consistently high for several years.

Pillows in Paradise has its own pool and is about a half mile outside of Kailua, but very close to grocery stores. It's run by Barbara High in her own home which gets great reviews.

Haleiwa

This town is on the North Shore, about an hour northwest of Honolulu. Home of Sunset Ranch and Sunset Beach Park, Haleiwa and Laniakea Beach, Waimea Valley, and so much more, it's another quiet option with tons of activities on offer.

Kalani Hawaii Private Lodging is run by Bernie and Maria Ines. It's another private house with a garden, kitchen, which is a stone's throw away from the Pipeline and Sunset beaches. It's pretty much a backpacker's place with a very laid-back atmosphere. If you need to get picked up from the airport, Bernie can do that for $85, which is cheaper than any shuttle service available.

HOTELS

If you'd rather go for hotels in Honolulu, the following top the list for cheap hotels at great locations and good value.

Waikiki Prince offers apartments with kitchenettes right beside Waikiki Beach and within walking distance from several attractions. They offer little else in terms of amenities, but get good reviews from those on a budget who prefer to be at the center of things.

Royal Grove Hotel is a mom-and-pop run outlet with kitchenettes. The place is a little higher-end, no frills, but is a great location near the beach and the Hawaii Convention Center.

Aqua Waikiki Wave is on the higher end for those who want a bit more, but don't want to dig into their pockets too deeply. It's also near Waikiki Beach, only one block away.

The Equus Hotel has great reviews for price, perks, and location. Ala Moana Blvd. is a trendy area of Waikiki and therefore busy, so it can be noisy.

Hotel Renew is a small boutique hotel right across Waikiki Beach. Despite its location, however, it gets high praise for price, though there's little in the way of amenities.

Waikiki Parc Hotel is right next to the Sheraton but charges a fraction of their price. Not much of a view unless you like seeing the Sheraton, but you can see the beach from the pool. While it is in Waikiki, you're not too close to all the action, so it's a lot quieter.

LUXURY STAYS

Halekulani means "House Befitting Heaven," which probably explains their prices, but it's on Waikiki Beach, so you can't beat the views. Deemed the finest hotel in the district, it's another institution, as it was set up in 1883. Despite their prices, the staff are renowned for their friendliness and warmth.

Chapter 3: Where to Eat and Drink

Hawaii is an incredible melting pot of peoples and cuisines. Besides American and European fare, it also boasts an incredible variety of local Polynesian grub together with Chinese, Japanese, Korean, Filipino, and Portuguese food.

KAHALA is an upscale district just outside Honolulu, so dining here is not generally cheap. You do get what you pay for, and that includes a generous helping of authentic Hawaiian charms.

Kona Brewing Co. specializes in local artisan beers. They also serve pizzas, barbecues, and salads. They have an outdoor dining area which is perfect on cool evenings.

Arancino at Kahala Resort serves high-end Italian cuisine with a modern twist. A very posh place, a four-course meal for one will set you back between $85 and $100 (minus tax and tips).

Town is a bistro and wine place that's been decorated to look like an art gallery, and has been getting rave reviews on the international scene.

Bogart's Café is on Monsarrat Avenue in a tiny mall, but is one of the cheaper options in this district. It's a coffee shop which serves vegetarian options. Their acai bowls are a particular favorite and costs about $9. This café only takes cash payments, no credit cards accepted.

Roy's is owned by celebrity chef Roy Yamaguchi, famous for his Eurasian blends. One of his dishes alone can set you back about $40, excluding drinks and everything else, but he's got the awards to prove they're worth it. His soufflés are to die for, by the way.

Canabas Seaside Grill, **Plumeria Beach House**, and **Hoku's** are three other award-winning dining options in the Kahala Hotel & Resort located right next to the beach. The prices are high, but worth it.

Olive Tree Café specializes in Middle Eastern cuisine, though their sign says "Mostly Greek Food." Their prices are on the lower end, despite having little competition for their theme in the Kahala area.

Café Laufer is a multi-award winning establishment renowned for their pastries, including local delicacies like the macadamia nut pie. They also serve great meals.

EAST SIDE comprises Laie, Kailua, Kaneohe, and Waimanalo. This is the greenest part of the island with some of the most spectacular scenery wedged between the mountains and the sea.

Hukilau Cafe lies near the North Shore and specializes in local cuisine. It's a favorite among residents, specializing in breakfast and lunch. The place is very small, however, and always packed. When you get in make your way to the counter and put your name on the list they give. Step back out and wait for your name to be called. The place was featured in "50 First Dates," with Drew Barrymore and Adam Sandler.

Heeia Pier General Store and Deli is a tiny waterfront restaurant in Kaneohe with great dishes, amazing views, fresh seafood, and locally grown beef. The menu selection is not big, but they pride themselves on freshness and affordable prices.

Haleiwa Joe's at Haiku Gardens is higher end, but the food and Japanese garden setting are unbeatable. The restaurant has great views of the Ko'olau Mountain Range, and you're welcome to tour the large premises which include a pond.

Uncle Bobo's Smoked BBQ specializes in Asian cuisine and barbecues on Kaaawa along Kamehameha highway.

They're a small roadside-type restaurant, so their prices are very affordable.

Keneke's Plate Lunch & BBQ has no indoor dining options, but is a local favorite on Waimanalo along Kalanianaole highway. Order your meal at the window and find yourself a table in the picnic area. Food portions are smaller than standard however.

Serg's Mexican Kitchen Nalo is also in Waimanalo and quite small. Their specialty is the huevos rancheros served on weekends.

Buzz's Original Steakhouse is on the windward side of Kailua Beach. They're a chain restaurant, but their food is consistently top notch. Bit expensive, though.

Polynesian Cultural Center Luau does luaus in bulk (1,200 people in one go!), and visiting Hawaii without experiencing a luau is a capital offense. Located in Laie, they also perform cultural dances and other local stuff, but it's run by Mormons, so no alcohol.

KAPOLEI is a resort town on the western part, halfway between North Shore and Honolulu. The area's a tad pricey, however, precisely because of those resorts.

Assagio Kapolei is an Italian restaurant that's casual but elegant with rather decent prices and generous portions. They also have a wine bar.

Ushio-Tei at the Marriot serves traditional Japanese food in a traditional Japanese garden setting. They have buffet meals starting at 5:30pm, but they do have a dress code.

Ama'ama is part of the Aulani Disney Resort & Spa right along the beach with open air seating. They specialize in Hawaiian and Asian cuisine, as well as local artisan beers.

Cattle Company Steakhouse upholsters its seats with black-and-white cowhide, so you know what you're getting. Besides their steak, they're also famous for their deserts, while their carrot cakes are to die for.

Down to Earth All Vegetarian Organic & Natural is the only vegetarian option on the island with three branches. It's a grocery which also serves meals and an all-day salad bar.

Thai Kitchen is owned and operated by a Thai family. They don't serve alcohol, but they do allow you to BYOB.

Paradise Cove Luau does the song and dance with luau, and they also have other cultural activities available. They're not Mormons, so they do serve alcohol in case you were wondering.

WAIKIKI is the main tourist drag, and there's a wide variety of establishments and price ranges to choose from.

Chart House has been around since 1969, the brainchild of famed surfer, Joey Cabell. It's therefore become an institution for surfers located right along the Ala Wai Harbor. The food is continental, and while posh, prices are well below resort standards.

Kobe Japanese Steak House & Sushi Bar is also sports a bar and a lively teppanyaki corner.

Pineapple Room is the restaurant of the Macy's mall, so while it's posh, prices vary from the high end to the affordable.

Orchids has fantastic views of Diamond Head, serving American, Continental, and Japanese cuisine. Their breakfasts are renowned, and their Sunday Brunch receives consistent awards.

Michels is a high end French chain that serves very traditional French food, with live music at night. Dress is semi-casual, but reservations are a must.

Irifune provides Japanese food served at home. Low key and no frills, but delicious, with prices that don't hurt.

Chapter 4: Best Places to Hike

With its spectacular scenery, hiking is one of the best ways to see the island. The raw beauty of untouched natural resources experienced up close cannot be compared. Note that some areas are occasionally closed off because of weather conditions or landslides, so check ahead before putting your hiking gear on.

Olomana Trail

With incredible views over Kailua, this spans some 2½ miles, nestled between the mountains and the sea. It's about 1.5 miles to the first of the three peaks which rise 1,000 feet high. It's not an easy trail, however, and is recommended only for serious hikers.

There's a bit of rock climbing involved so ropes have been provided to access the first peak. Once you get to the top, it's very narrow and can accommodate only a few people at a time. For most hikers, the thrill of the hike up to this point is enough. For the more adventurous, the trail toward the other two peaks lies ahead.

Diamond Head Summit Trail

The Diamond Head volcano's crater is some 3,500 feet in diameter. You start in the middle and make your way toward the rim some 560 feet up, a distance of some 1.6 miles. You'll find some steep stairs toward a tunnel which leads you to the top. The bunkers there were built during World War II, but now house a communications array for the government. There are no facilities past the starting point, so bring your own water or buy some from the stands.

Waihee Ridge Trail

This spans 4½ miles in the West Maui Forest Reserve. Not at all steep, but this is in the wettest part of the island with lush vegetation and lots of mud. There are many beautiful waterfalls, however, worthy of lots and lots of pictures.

Makapu'u Point Lighthouse Trail

This is an easy trail on the Ka Iwi State Scenic Shoreline stretching some 2 miles to Moloka'I and Lana'i. The months of November and May are the perfect time to see the whale migration, if you're lucky.

Manoa Falls

The trail's muddy but easy, so wear sturdy shoes. This is where they filmed *Lost* and *Jurassic Park*, so you already know what to expect. They have toilets en route, so you don't have to fertilize the already lush vegetation.

Wa'ahila Ridge Trail

This is moderately difficult and spans 1.8 miles. It starts at the Wa'ahila state park atop St. Louis Heights and goes all the way to Mt. Olympus. Past that point is not recommended for those not fit or experienced, as it requires some rock climbing.

Manana Trail

This is near Pearl City, a county of Honolulu to the north of Pearl Harbor. Stretching some 4 miles, it's relatively flat and good for jogs. There are no provisions for water here, so bring your own.

Kapiolani Park, Diamond Head, and Kapahulu

This is actually a city park stretching some 7.2 miles across three districts. Along the way, you can enjoy some sporting facilities, as well as cultural venues, such as the Honolulu Zoo, Waikiki Aquarium, and more.

Kuli'ou'ou Ridge Trail

The trail starts at the bottom of the ridge then stretches some 2.25 miles to rise some 1,800 feet. It's steep, but worth the great views. There are no toilets or water facilities, but there is a picnic area halfway up.

Chapter 5: Best Places to Bike

There are plenty of cycling options throughout the island. If you don't want to bring your own bicycle, there are many companies that provide rentals — some even provide tours on them.

Oahu is one of the most bike-friendly territories in America, and even Honolulu has quite a number of bicycle trails. Many of these lead to other parts of the island, including hiking trails.

Diamond Head Crater

There's a bike route that stretches from Waikiki along Kapahulu Avenue, goes around the Diamond Head Crater to the top, then back down to Kahala. It isn't actually necessary to bike to the top of the crater, but the views are worth it.

Manoa Falls Bike & Hike

This starts at Kapahulu Avenue where the bike path begins. The trail passes through various city spots like the Ala Wai Golf Course and the University of Hawaii Manoa. The route continues on to the Manoa Falls Trail where you have to hike. You can also pass by the Lyon Arboretum or head on toward Diamond Head.

Waikiki and Magic Island

This is a more urban route designed to let you see more cultural venues like the US Army Museum and the Ala Moana Beach Park. Magic Island is an artificial peninsula that juts from the park and is a posh place for yachts.

Pearl Harbor Bike Path

This starts past the Pearl Harbor Marina and ends at the Waipi'o Point Access Road. There are a number of wooden bridges to cross, and while a number of points are interesting, the rest are through industrial portions of the city.

Pupukea Trail

For mountain bike enthusiasts, this one is a challenge not meant for novices. Its 14 miles of muddy uphill terrain, but the downhill ride is incredible.

Kealia Trail

This leads to the Peacock Flats on top where picnic facilities are available. The trail is very narrow and so steep in some places that you'll have to get off your bike and walk. The views, however, are well worth it.

Chapter 6: Top Five Beaches for Surfing, Swimming, and Snorkeling

Beaches are what Hawaii is associated with, but remember that not all are suitable for swimming. Based on popularity, the following make up the top five beaches in the island, where you can swim, surf, and snorkel your Hawaii days away.

Lanikai Beach

You'll find this in Kailua, one of the most beautiful of the island's many beaches. Thanks to offshore reefs, the waters here are calm throughout the year, making it great for swimming, kayaking, sailing, and windsurfing. The waters are crystal clear all year long, also making it ideal for snorkeling.

Kailua Beach Park

This is about a mile away from Lanikai Beach and has been dubbed one of Hawaii's best. Water clarity extends three miles out, while reefs keep it generally calm. Windsurfing's good, but the low waves make it unsuited for surfing. Since it's very popular, it tends to be more crowded.

Waimanalo Bay Beach Park

This stretches from Wailea Point to Makapuu, a distance of about five miles, making it the longest beach on Oahu. The waters are rougher here, making it great for surfing, but not so great for swimmers. The fishing is great, though.

Waikiki Beach

This is the world-famous city beach, crammed with tourists, resorts, and shops. Because the waters are protected, they're generally calm, making them ideal for swimming and canoeing, but water visibility is not so good for snorkeling. High waves further out make surfing possible. Be sure to visit the Honolulu Zoo and Waikiki Aquarium nearby.

Sunset Beach

Located in the North Shore, the waters are obscenely blue, calm, and absolutely clear during summer. This is the time for swimming, snorkeling, and kayaking. Winter is when the waves rise, making it the ideal season for surfing. Please note that waves here are so high that only very experienced surfers are advised to try it out.

Chapter 7: Exploring the Local History

In addition to its natural beauty, Oahu has a lot of culture to offer. It is too numerous to mention here, but some of the must-see places include the following.

Pearl Harbor

This historic site is still a military base that hosts several museums. It takes an entire day to see all of the exhibits, so plan your visit accordingly. Do note that since 911, security has been tightened, which delays the lines, somewhat Be sure to also visit the USS Arizona Memorial and the USS Missouri.

Iolani Palace

Hawaii used to be an independent kingdom 'til it was absorbed by the US. This palace housed the last local monarch, Queen Liliuokalani, who lived there till 1893.

Bishop Museum and Planetarium

This is a great place to see Hawaiian culture before its absorption into the US. Other artifacts come from cultures which define it today, including those brought by early Asian and European settlers.

Mission Houses Museum

These restored houses were the residences of the first missionaries to the islands. It was here that they translated the bible into the local language and disseminated it, often through force, upon the natives.

Polynesian Cultural Center

They don't just have great luaus, they also do what they can to preserve Polynesian culture, of which Hawaiian culture is a part. Despite the touristy atmosphere, there is a genuine attempt to preserve what's left of its heritage, complete with a Polynesian village, exhibits, and other activities.

Finally, I'd like to thank you for purchasing this book! If you enjoyed it or found it helpful, I'd greatly appreciate it if you'd take a moment to leave a review on Amazon. Thank you!

55301355R00030

Made in the USA
Lexington, KY
17 September 2016